Against Starlight

Anton Knox Elder

5 Fold Media
Visit us at www.5foldmedia.com

Against Starlight

Published by 5 Fold Media, LLC
www.5foldmedia.com

For bulk orders of twenty (20) or more books, contact 5 Fold Media by email sales@5foldmedia.com or call 315-314-6480.

ISBN: 978-1-936578-72-6

Library of Congress Control Number: 2013943062

Dedication

For Susan,

Whose love and encouragement

has kept Jesus

close to my heart through both

joyous and tragic times.

Without her love and support,

inspired by Christ,

this work would not be published.

Contents

In the Garden Alone

there
in the dark garden
sits a
contemplative soul
talking to His Father
begging for answers
to questions
that in everlasting love
through anguish
a stirring heart knows
as a shadow of light
gathers on half a face
an eye staring
into the vastness
then turning with a crushed heart
speaks what those sleeping would not hear
let your will, not mine, be done.

White Clouds

When eagles
touch the sky,
soft blueness
in white clouds,
we lift our hearts
in Holy Prayers
of thankfulness.

On this
soft earth
Christ came
and suffered
so that in the crispness
of being
we could find
salvation.

The flight of eagles
touching the sky
of white clouds,
filling us full
of joyful prayers
for God.

Mighty Miracle

Pray constantly
with a contrite heart.
Lift up all with love
and God will create
a mighty miracle!

No Greater Gift

If you love Christ,
speak it.
"I love Jesus;
He is my Savior."

Loving is giving
no greater Gift
than to open another's heart
to Jesus
simply by
praising,
speaking out,
shouting,
yelling!
"I love Jesus;
He is my Savior."

Do not hide Christ.
Share Him with the world!
What a blessing.
A blessing to others,
and a blessing to you.

The Light

The light of
darkness
begins
to fade
to vanish
when you
ind Jesus
The pure
Light of Salvation.

Vision

Praying with others,
the Spirit
        of the Lord
opened my heart
and it sang out:
"Praise God,
      Praise Him."
As I was overcome
by the Holy Spirit
pulling me out of
      the darkness
into the Light,
      there was
a vision of
Jesus walking,
      in white garments,
bearded. His kind eyes
      looking at us
as He
      approached us
holding a lantern
      out in front of Him,
      smiling warmly.
      Suddenly
our prayers came to life—
                lifted, lifted
                    up to Him.

Peace and Joy

To live, know, and obey Christ
will give you Peace and Joy...

Peace and Joy.

Amen.

God's Eternal Glory

always
    remain humble
read His Word
        pray to Him
        in worship
        alone and
          with a multitude
witness to others
        reach out
          bring others home
bring them to Christ
  by softening hearts
       so that God
          can call them
    into His arms
    where they can find
         peace and rest
         in His Eternal Glory.

Hold God Close

Bow down and pray.
Hold God close;
Not as Someone you know
but as Someone you Love—

Our Lord Jesus Christ.

God Watches Over You

As a small
   child sleeps
you can see the peace
            the restfulness
and know an angel
         is watching over her
and
as you are there
         loving the child
realize too
         that God is also
         watching over you.

Victorious

we rise
into the sun
victorious
      for
we are
      His.

Safe

Newly saved,
   or many years saved,
the safest place for
   a Christian
is in the Bible.
   Praying? Yes,
but the best is
   by rejoicing and
   praising
   our Sweet Lord
         in worship
where all are
         lifted
            In Jesus' joy.

Church

Attend church
and listen—

listen to the sermon
for it is a light into the darkness.

Fall to Your Knees

Fall to your knees—
it is no time to pray sweetly,
for Satan is not timid.
He tears into weakened hearts
with pain
and illness,
addiction
and horror.
He stirs the coals of hell
while you softly whisper.

Yes, a whisper will drive Satan away.
So just imagine
the power of loud,
knee-driven
prayer
attacking Satan.

Drive Satan out, Jesus.
Destroy his evil works.

For the victory is ours
in Christ we are victorious!

Healing Love

Jesus, hold our loved ones close.
Keep the forces of Your voice
within them.
Heal them, Lord—
their hearts,
their essence.
We pray, Sweet Jesus,
that You flood them with Your
healing love.

Amen.

Freely Given

through moments
with the Lord
God our Father
we are lifted
transformed

always find
time

moments of perfection
to fall on your knees
and in worship
be thankful
for the fullness
the joy
the love
He has given you
freely.

Praise God

With each blessed
moment you breathe,

Praise God! Praise God!

The Breath We Breathe

So blessed are we
for the very view
of the blue sky above us
the clouds in wisps of white
the grass wet beneath our feet
the warmth of the Sun
so blessed are we for God's presence
all around us

Thank You Lord Jesus
for the breath we breathe
and for saving us from our sins
with Your blood.

Amen.

Shine

Allow the Light of God
to shine
through you
into the world.

The Forgiveness of Jesus

Once saved, under grace,
I asked Jesus for forgiveness—
He said, "I forgive you."

I asked Jesus to forgive me,
He replied, "You are forgiven—go."

I asked Jesus for forgiveness,
"For what?" Jesus asked.

I told Him.
He said, "I have no memory
of that sin."

But still I begged, forgive me Jesus!
He again said, "For what?"
I told Him.

"I have no memory of you sinning,"
He said.

I could feel a smile.
I could feel His warm and beautiful love.
I understood
I was the only one who could
remember.

But not the only one.

Someone—more like something—
does remember me sinning—
was helping me remember my sins.

Now, with a smile on my face
from a warm and loving heart—
the heart of my Savior—
I could not remember anymore either
for I claimed
the forgiveness of Jesus.

Everlasting

Lifting
my hands
upward
I felt Christ's hand
gathering
my heart, now
full of grace,
as tears
poured down
my cheeks
drowning
me in complete love—
the precious blood
of the Lamb
now in freedom
my voice sings
to my Father God
His Presence
through Christ
mine
everlasting.

Amen!

Lift and Fly

Across each heart
whose hurt lays heavy,
is an answer:
a way to rise,

to lift,
to fly.

That answer is Jesus.

The Nest

Upon the post of
  the old birdhouse,
I peered in
   on the gentle lift of
      my toes.

Fresh makings
   in the nest,
the sound of bluebirds,
filled my ears,
and gave me knowledge
   that soon,
in the sight of the
opening, would be
round, bluish eggs.

  Soon
    thereafter
to give flight
 on lifted wings.

How precious
  is each moment
  in God's world.

Anton Knox Elder

Sword of Righteousness

If there is
evil in your life
pray you fall upon
Christ's sword of
righteousness
piercing your heart with love and faith
and the acceptance that Christ
is the Son of God
raised to life by God His Father

then you are saved.

worship Him.
worship Him.

Open Heart

A closed heart
can do nothing;
but an open heart
with Christ
can do anything!

God's Loving Eyes

Without salvation,
life on this earth
is just life
clothed in flesh—
so lost, lost
in death.

There is no
transformation
to calmness,
love, or peace,
no uplifting
of people's spirits.

No prayer for miracles.
No disciples.

Talents are misused:
None seek their
ministry
to save others.

Without salvation,
death is sure
and certain,

but
with Christ,
there is eternal life
and transformation.

We are new,
we are joyful,
we are worshiping,
we are soaring.
Up...
Up...
Uplifted

looking into God's loving
eyes.

Bliss

Lift your saddened heart
to God
and let Him in.
Let Jesus in.
Then joy, the Holy Spirit,
and God
will fill your heart
with bliss.

Worship Him

Call them,
call them to Jesus.
Keep your heart open,
and help to open theirs
so all will
worship Him.

Lifted

God gracefully
        lifted His hand
and day
        by day
all that is
        and was
and is going to be
touched our hearts
touched our souls
and by His hand
      we are lifted
          we are His
               we are saved.

Heaven

to find
    forever
hope and joy
to know forever
heaven is our home
we need only believe
that Christ is Lord
and the risen Son of God
then we are sure
  our home is heaven
  no matter what
    we may face
        in this world.

Worship God

The sun opened up
this morning
on God's glorious creation
and I thought,
felt,
experienced,
His love,
and could not
in any way know,
understand,
how anyone could not
be humbled,
falling at the feet of Jesus our Lord
in awesome worship!

Me

How much joy
and abundance
do we have?

How could any thought of
"me"
become significant

when so many blessings
are constantly flowing?

Praise God!

Praise God!

Amen, Amen, Praise God!

Broken

It is hard
when your essence
is broken
it is hard to be broken

But sin is in and
through
this world
and we in humbleness
do pray
for wholeness

and Jesus freely gives it
but it may still be broken

the body giving into sin

it breaks down

it can be hurt

but it can be healed
by faith, by promise

but still on this earth
it dies
even Lazarus raised, died again

But Lazarus, like us who are saved,
could and did choose
eternal life in the Kingdom

so we may not be healed
but we can be saved

God can do anything He wants
but you might be broken
and it is hard
because we want to be strong
and powerful as others seem to be
we want to do all the things
those who are able do

but we must remember
because of who we are
to always be witnesses for Jesus
we are saved
blessed with eternal life
and we must share with others not saved
so they can be blessed

we are human now
eternal now
and eternal always
by Christ's sacrifice on the cross

so if we must endure, we must remember
what Christ endured

we who are Christians know
this life is short
as if a flicker of light

we know the things others do
on this earth
are momentary

we will be perfect
we will rise
we will be with Christ

but as humans
on this planet
we suffer

but as Christians
with glorious life eternal
we know eternity in
perfection
is coming

but simply
it is hard
to deal with the limitations
of a broken body
and in praying, for healing,
miracles do come
miracles abound

but we know in our hearts
the glorious day will come
when this body we will lay down
and rise in perfection
in the Kingdom of the Lord
so, don't give up

even if you have to live

with a broken body
Witness
Witness
and Rejoice!

Amen.

In Prayer

lift your lostness
    to Jesus
and He will
    touch you
    strengthen you
and bring you home
    to Him
    to everlasting peace
    and love.

All I Am

Understand
all I am
is His.

God's Lamb

Saved!

Baptized!

An infant in Christ has been born!

But without uplifting guidance,
without reading the Bible,
without attending Church,
without Praying
and Worshiping God,
this new lamb will never grow.

So find them, guide them,
read the Bible to them,
go to Church with them,
pray and worship God with them.

Give them direction to
God's people—
God's love—
So they may grow and be a
blessing to all.

Eternal Life

I reached out for the hand of
Christ—
He reached back with
eternal life.

The Misguided

There is
that sadness
when a child
full of faith
is driven
unknowingly away
from Christ
by those who are lost
and misguided.
The battle is
to pray and minister,
to pull the child
back toward grace—
toward Christ—
and to guide
those lost toward salvation.

Pray for the softening of
hardened hearts
and give this
child every flight
to God.
The child loves God
and
God is in the child's heart.

We pray profoundly, in earnestness,
for their salvation.

Prayer

each moment
you breathe prayer
is a moment
of true blessings!

Amazing

It is amazing
    What the Lord can do
When faithful people
        Let Him loose!

When God's people
    Let Him loose
Amazing things happen!

When faithful people
    Let God loose,
Amazing things get done!

Let God loose!

Run

Seek not
to hide from Jesus.
Run.
Run into His arms.

Without Light

To be lost
and not know Jesus
is to be without light
in pitch darkness.
The beauty though
is that others who know you
pray for you;
and the dazzling light
of the Lord Jesus
blinds you
with His beauty,
saving you
through His kind
and gentle Spirit.

The Wind

Catch the wind in your sail.
Trust in God
and hold on!

Awaken

We who believe
        must awaken.
For You are constantly
                orchestrating
                        our lives:
keeping us,
        loving us,
                guiding us.
We must awaken
        and realize;
            we must confess
                our paths
                    to others

so they will follow
        and awaken to Your
        truth and love.
            And, being saved,
awaken
    bringing,
        bringing,
            others to You.

Faith That Soars

Blessed are they
whose faith soars!

Crying Child

And if you see a child crying
you comfort them
you reach out to them
you console them.

Why any less for a child...
any child of God of any age!

Reach out.
Comfort them, console them,
tell them the Good News.
Tell them the story of salvation;
love them as God has loved you!

Peace

Allow Jesus into your heart
and the "peace that passes all
understanding"
will be yours.

Family of Christ

Don't wait!
    Who knows when the
        heart stops?
Invite Jesus, Son of God,
    into your heart
        and transform
        into the family of Christ.

Forever Safe

when you see
the awesome universe
the stars and
beyond the stars
beyond forever
remember that
the breath of God
is what keeps you safe
forever safe

Father
breathe on us, breathe on us.

Amen.

In His Hands

What moment
in your life
did you begin
to find calmness and peace

When you began to love Christ
when you began to read His Word
When you began to turn the
noise and fear
sadness and loneliness
over to Him
When you began to grow in faith
laying the pains of the world
in His Hands.

His Presence

Do you understand
the thunder of
His presence?

Witness to Others

If you have a moment
to be there for others
let it be real
let it be of
and through Jesus
keeping your presence
in His Love
helping
praying
witnessing
to others.

All Eternity

Having been saved
    you belong to God:
     not just now,
          not just today,
               not just tomorrow,
     but for
          all eternity.

Come into My Heart

My heart sweeps
outward
seeking His
praying to Him
to my Jesus
come Jesus
come into my heart
come Jesus
be within me
me within You
transformed
forevermore
transformed
eternally
bursting in praise
growing in faith
seeking ever
closer to You
to our Father God
to the Holy Spirit
seeking
praying
come, come into my heart
forever come
let my heart
cling ever closer
to You.

Amen.

Pray Each Day

Pray each day
to God.
Pray each day.

Courage

Sitting there
in a seat on Sunday
a calling
calling me
and although I was frightened
I found the courage
the courage to answer
There I was
no longer seated
drifting
finding myself
at the altar
with my preacher

Accept Jesus as your Savior
the Only Son of God
and ask forgiveness for your sins

There on my knees
somehow on my knees
my heart burst with joy
as I heard my Savior say

Yes, you are saved
you are forgiven
you are My child.

Forgiven

In the presence of God's Love
all things are forgiven.

Saved

To become whole, seek Jesus,
seek God.
Be flooded with the Holy Spirit.
Simply say,
        "Come into my heart, Lord,
          come into my heart."
Believe
        with all in you
that Jesus is the true Son of God:
                                        The Living God.
Then shake off sin
                        and be free
        for the rest of your existence;
not just now,
                        not just a moment,
                            but eternally.

Not for Me

When you are lost,
confused,
don't know what to do,
pray this:

Dear Jesus,
not for me
but for You.
Let Your will be done.

Amen.

Not a Cloud in the Sky

We live in darkness:
thick, swirling darkness
full of pain,
and greed,
covetness, crudeness,
ungodly desires,
worship of self, arrogance.
Thick, swirling darkness,
choking the life out of us.
Without Him—
and Him alone—
we are lost; lost in this
possessive storm of pitch blackness.

Lost,
until we open our hearts
and call out to our
Savior.
Repenting of our sins
we suddenly see our Jesus
in a clear, blue sky,
and are
filled with His light,
joy, and worship.

Holy Ground

Touch nothing else but Holy Ground.
Do you understand? Nothing else
but other than to drive Satan out!

Pour

Do not
stand in despair
in sadness
in depression
lift your arms
fall on your knees
and shout
take me Jesus
take me
I invite you
into my heart
forgive me
accept me
take me
love me
accept me
fill me with the
love You have been
pouring over me
all my life
I see it
feel it flowing
I invite You into
my heart
so that filled
I might
pour Your love
over others.

Heart of Faith

Where can we find a
heart
of love, of purpose,
of faith?

Jesus.

Bring Them Home

Once saved
become God's.
Read the Scriptures,
learn many by heart,
for your heart is open.

Pray to Jesus;
Sing to Jesus.
Praise Him.
Worship Him
by attending church
with others
so that you might grow,
strengthened,
in the Spirit,
so you will witness,
touching others,
spreading the Good News.

Then the Light of Jesus
will spread,
spread to the lost,
bringing them Home.

Every Moment

Every moment
is a moment to
praise God.

Amen.

The Hands of God

Saddened by the pain
        of those around us
we must fall
        upon our knees
        and pray
for those in pain
                and anguish
        then
we must lift up
        gather ourselves
                and go to
those we have prayed for
                humbly
        to be the hands of God
            to begin their healing
        and ours.

Love

Lift up your loved ones.
Hold them and
love them with all your heart
as Jesus loves you.

Teach them to love one another
as Jesus loves them.

Worship

Worship God, the Father
Worship Jesus, our Savior
        Worship Him
pray to Him
        sing Him songs of praise
        with those who love Him
seek the Holy Spirit
        read the Bible
Worship Him
        for in this Way
you will grow
        you will transform
and waking
        you will find Him in your heart
        in your everyday life.

The Answer

And I asked,
"How can I have
love, peace, and joy?"
And the answer
rested gently upon me:
"By staying in God's hands."

All

If your family is lost,
gather them up on Sunday,
and
take them to
God's House
where God's Love
will
fill your family
and you
with togetherness
with joy
with respect
and all
will be blessed by Jesus
with not just love and fulfillment
but with eternal life.

Lift Up Your Children

I pray.

I pray
that you will lift up your children
and, without
delay,
deliver them into the
sweet, loving arms of Jesus!

Amen!

Sadness

Do not let
    sadness
        pour continually into
    your life
Open your eyes
    look heavenward
    and pray simple forgiveness
    then rise and walk
    against sin
        Do not let it rise again.

Against Starlight

Imagine
    Imagine
        Imagine
Christ in Heaven...

Imagine
    in the darkness of night
    stars bright against God's sky,
    Joseph and Mary
    weary, seeking a place of rest
    gathered now against the time of birth
    into a manger

And there
among the soft sounds of
sheep and goats...
Joseph, now looking up
    toward heaven
as Mary begins labor

Imagine Christ
    in Heaven...
Our Creator, to have been, to always be
    and now against the night
    in Bethlehem
    born under angels' wings
    breaking all silence
    crying as if to the Father

Christ on earth
Christ on earth

Soon a small child learning
how to carve and mold wood
not only wood
but soon to mold men
to touch their hearts
to forgive their sins
to be about His Father's work

He saw sacrifice
imagine
Jesus watching sacrifices
participating in
sacrifices as He grew

Then
John the Baptist
born under Angels
submerged Christ
and as He rose from the water

"*This is My* Beloved *Son*, in *Whom I am* well pleased!"[1]

Imagine
Christ on earth
leading the Way
teaching us to care for one another
healing us
guiding us to truth
but above all showing us love and forgiveness

1. Mark 1:11 NKJV

Then in clear authority
but with tears and prayers
He rose to be crucified

This Gift
our greatest gift
His sacrifice
to be betrayed
to choose to be torn
ripped
nailed in agony to the cross
as mutterings, curses and gambling rose
from below

Imagine... no, we cannot imagine this
nor conceive
what Love this is

Imagine
Christ in Heaven
as Mary settled in the manger
as Wise Men
sought Him by following
God's shining star
So that you and I can
Live and Thrive in the beauty of this world
having been blessed in Christ
having been given eternal life
by simply, fully, faithfully
accepting Christ as God's only begotten son

Imagine
    Christ doing so
    with tears in His eyes
    Love in His heart
    fully forgiving us

    Imagine.
    Imagine.

    Amen.

Bring Glory

Worship Him, yes
love Him truly
for He died for your sins
so you would be saved
forgiven of your sins
bring glory to His Name
through your actions
through your works
that saved, you would witness
telling others the Good News
bringing others to salvation
bring glory
to His Name
our sweet Lord Jesus.

In His Arms

Christ,
gently
hold us in your arms
and let us know
that we are Yours.

Amen.

Little One

Do not pull
        on the shoulder
of a Christian child
        or any child
and turn their eyes toward
            emptiness
lest you fall
            into eternal darkness
as you have endangered
        the soul of a
        child's heart
            that loves Christ
let all children go to Him
        take all children to Him.

Light

Against darkness is light:
Do not live in the darkness,
seek the Light.
The Light is Jesus.

Amen.

Son of Man

Eve after Adam
Satan forbidden
Prophets
Kings
Mary
God's Baby
John
dove
my Son in whom
I am well pleased

tempted... sinless
teacher
healer
Son of Man

crucifixion
death
Jesus raised by God
sin defeated
Satan's power lost
ascension
Holy Spirit flows in baptism
Light
Jesus returns
the earth imbibes
Satan into lake of fire
new earth
grace eternal

Rise

sadness
　　　lostness
loneliness
　　　　tears
　　　　　　evaporate
as prayers
　　　　rise
to our sweet Lord Jesus.

Understand the Good News

There is nowhere to
fall if you are
uplifted
transformed
from a child
who sees the Good News
to an adult
who understands
the Good News
who loves and worships
Jesus as their true Lord.

The Creator

In the dark of night
    look on God's creation
look at the stars
            the planets
            the galaxies
for they are worshiping
        their Creator
        our Father God.

Complete Love

There can be joy
in your life;
there can be complete love.
Lift up your heart;
pray for Jesus to enter
your heart.
Accept His Light
to banish your sins
and know
grace is your companion
and that the Spirit of Christ
is with your soul.
You are saved.
You are God's.
For as you
were dead
you are now alive!
You are transformed
into beauty.
Praise Him, praise Him.

Now saved, now sanctified,
go out and spread
the Good News
to all you know.
Love them as Jesus loves you!

A Clean Heart

keep your heart clean
        and your life will be
                                a joy
not only for you
                    but all others
                          who know you.

Shout the Good News

Do not hide there
in the shadows,
your hands in your pockets,
moving timidly around.

Step up!
Step out!
Stare Satan down.

Christ has already been victorious!

So with the voice of Good News,
show them.
With God's Word,
flood them with the Holy Spirit
Allow Grace—
God's sweet Grace—
so they too can become part of God's Kingdom!

Do not hide there in the shadows
with your hands in your pockets!
Shout the Good News!

God Will Fill Your Heart

God fills the oceans
        God fills the earth
and
      with His Light
He will fill your heart.

Redeemer

People
readers of the Bible
do you understand
 do you feel
He taught phenomenally!
 Amazingly! Awesomely!
Healed the blind, the meek,
 the lame, anyone in need!
Called demons out
 raised the dead
and chose to be crucified for our sins
 because He loves us so
      died and was raised again
 by His Father
       sent us the Holy Spirit
       to guide us
 toward His Light
         toward eternal Life
Wonderful, Amazing, truly He is the
Son of God.

This Hard Heart of Mine

As in His gentle, lifting hand
He moved
this hard heart of mine
softly forgiven
now full of love and joy
He saved through sacrifice
this hard heart of mine.

Praise

Lift your eyes.
Raise your arms.
Praise our Lord Jesus.

Shout!
Sing!
Cry!

For you are saved
by grace.
For you opened your heart
and confessed
that Jesus is Lord,

is the Son of God.

Lift your eyes.
Raise your arms.
Praise our Lord Jesus.
For you are saved;
you are
a child of God.

Service

If we want to serve others
we must first
allow Christ into our hearts
as our Savior
and then serve Him.

"I"

"I need this..."
"I need that..."
"They hurt me..."
"I deserve..."
"I want..."
"They have things..."
"Where is mine?"

These are dreams
of the flesh—
whispers of Satan.

Push away
these thoughts, let them go!

Leave your needs to God.
He loves you;
He will care for you.
Be thankful for all there is.
Praise God for all you have.
Seek to help others,
to lift them up,
and you will find
your life fulfilled.

Forgive Us

Forgive us, Lord Jesus
For we know not
what we do—

forgive us our sins.

Amen.

Teach Your Children

Whoever you are,
wherever you are,

teach your children
to pray the Lord's Prayer
and to say the twenty-third Psalm.
Teach them the Ten Commandments,

witness constantly to them
every day in everything.

At night hold their hands;
with family around
each pray for one another.

These are your promises to God;
neglect them not.

And you, as you read them the Bible
and take them to church,
will be Blessed beyond all measure!

Move

Listen to your heart
    reaching,
        reaching,
as God's presence
    reaches back.
Don't hesitate;
move, fall on your knees
    and pray forgiveness.
Let Him enter your heart forever.

God Loves You

Can you not see
the power of sin
so many hurt
both physically
and within their hearts

addictions
torn covenants
destroying God's bonds of marriage
leaving you lost

hurting hearts
getting separated
from loved ones
from God

loving hearts hardening
pushing away
God for sin
choosing to be alone
as sin drives your soul down in horror
dividing God from you
loved ones from you
in the living death you breathe.

you can
you must look
for God is seeking you
            to heal you
to bring you home to Him
            to your loved ones
in your distress, don't seek
        darkness by blaming Him
for sin is the power of evil
the destruction of your soul

rather, seek God who loves you
    loves you so much
    He gave His Son, Jesus
    crucified for your sins
    repent
        and be saved
    don't choose separation, hurting
    desolation of the very person
    God Loves
                you.

                    you.

                        Amen.

Mighty Trumpet

God has blessed us with:
Jesus
His love
prophets, Scriptures
the Bible
so that we find our way
through the darkness
to the Light
and in His Spirit help others
and lead all to Christ
who sacrificed His life
so that we might keep ours
who rose again, ascended
and will come for us
when the mighty trumpet sounds.

Amen.

Uplifted

Begin a new life;
a life uplifted.
Read John.
Read Ephesians.
Read your Bible, pray,
go to church,
sing,
and you will find
a new life
Uplifted.

Emptiness

There are many who dream
to be known as
powerful among men—
There are those who desire
fame, wealth, and respect while
here on this earth—
yet their hearts are false
commanding them into
eternal emptiness.

You can be fulfilled
in God
so do not seek to chase men
and their desires.
Reach out for our Lord Jesus
who will love you,
and within His heart,
invite you to Him.
For you, accepting Christ, will be saved.

Then,
then you will be reaching out for Him
leading others to a
free, forgiven,
and eternal life.

Explode Our Hearts

Let us not be lost
in ourselves—
in hardened hearts.
But if we are, Jesus,
we pray
You explode our hearts with
tenderness
so that through Your love
we are saved.

Amen.

Pain

Amid the agony
        of pain
is our Savior…

   our prayers uplifted
to the angels high,
   our hearts
   held round by the
   Holy Ghost,
our prayers are to Jesus,
                    to God,
   to Yahweh, prayed
   through faith
   we seek healing.
   But the true miracle was
        through torment, agony,
        through pain, separation
        already past:

The pain Christ suffered
on the cross…

With our sins forgiven,
what pain we have left is
witnessed by our true hearts

and, if not lifted before,
will be destroyed upon
        ascension.

Forever His

to close
your
heart
to Christ's promises
is to
leave life barren

I pray
you burst forth
into the morning's sunlight
and
allow
the truth
to be blended
into your heart
forever His.

Seek Jesus

Jesus is here
He is everywhere
everywhere

If you see darkness
open your
heart
Jesus is the Light
that moves toward you
in all that darkness

Jesus is here
can you see Him

Pray
for the Light is shining
chasing away
the darkness
there is Jesus, clear and beautiful

The world
cannot extinguish the Light.

Pray to Jesus
fall upon your knees
Repent
as you allow Jesus
accept Jesus
invite Jesus
into your happy heart
Jesus is
everywhere
always in your heart
Praise God, for you are saved.

Amen.

How Blessed

To be saved
    we only need believe
You are the Risen Son
of the Living God
        crucified
            for our Sins
sacrificed, punished:
            You are our Lord

How blessed
How blessed we are
We praise your Perfect Love.

Never Alone

Whatever dark road
no matter how lost
  you are never alone
Remember
  you are never alone
  God is there
      God is always with you
you are never
      never without God.

Eternal Love

Awaken no more in fear;
be no longer condemned.
Accept Christ
into your heart,
the only Son of the Living God:

accept the Light,
accept the Love,
transform from darkness
into beauty—
into a child of God.
Then seek
to love others
as Jesus has loved you.
Forget yourself,
no longer trip over yourself.

Fill the world around you with love,
the love of Christ.
In boldness
invite all to Christ—
invite them all
into God's eternal love;
His precious,
eternal love.

Precious,
Precious,
Eternal love.

The Mighty Sword of God

Lift

Lift

His mighty sword

The Word of the Lord
The Holy Bible.

The Prayer of a Hurting Heart

Jesus lift us up
let us realize our beauty
let us care for each other
let us be filled with joy

Help our hurting hearts, Jesus,
so that we may speak lovingly
to all who suffer
for all of us suffer

Help our hurting hearts, Jesus,
so that we may forgive others
as You forgive us

Jesus, lift us up
bring healing to our broken hearts
so that we may care for others
bring them joy
as You have cared
for us
and brought us joy.

Amen.

Overcome

Free yourself from all distractions
free yourself of all addiction
from all webs of Satan

Run with joy
cling to happiness
to Jesus
for in Him is the strength to
overcome.

Believers

Saved,
the faithful
must seek
to stand in the Light
and through the Light
to be filled with the Light
so that when we
        see others in
      darkness
our light,
        the Sprit of Christ,
invites them
        into the Light

As believers
we must have
        the courage
        to shine
   so darkness
                cannot remain
where Christ's Presence is

For where His believers are
        The Light is.

Salvation

Let us falter not
when we see another in need
Even before they see it
offer help

Offer a way for salvation
to open up in their heart
a way to Jesus
a way to love
a way to grace
the way to salvation
to Jesus
to Jesus Christ.

Wings of Faith

Give the good news
to your children
and praise God by teaching
them the Bible
so their faith will be
strong
and their armor powerful.
Yes, praise God with your children,
so they become the
wings of faith
that keeps evil at bay.

Your Child

When your child is
        gently lowered
                into the water
knowing
        Jesus' blood
        was shed for them
tears of
    endless
        joy and thankfulness
                flow.

Love One Another

to touch the heart of another
is to love them

to see them, to care for them
is to love them

to serve them, to be there for them
is to love them

to pray with them, to pray for them
is to love them

fully and completely

yes
yes, all these things
are love

before you even shake their hand
before you even stand in their presence
you are loving them
being there for them

blessed are those who love one another
fully, spiritually

before even a hello
before even a hug

"Love one another as I have loved you."[2]

2. John 13:34 NKJV.

Remain

If you have not already,
forget yourself.

Kneel down
  in a silent place
and
  in the quiet,
    no matter how strange,
    begin to speak.
  No matter how awkward
          you feel,
  talk and wait.
          Wait.
  Even when you stop
          talking,
  wait.
      Suddenly,
          a presence will
                be there.
      Stay still,
          listen,
 for God will be there,
    His presence will be there,
        love will be there.

    Stay;
        remain
 as your heart opens
            to God's presence.

Pray

Pray Hard
Pray Fast
Pray Humbly
Pray Constantly

For others to come to Christ!

Freedom

On my knees
I fall
as light from Heaven
showers down on me
causing great joy
casting grace
I pray to Jesus
worshipping Him
for my freedom
to ever be His.

Your Light

Open up the
sky, Jesus
and in Your Light
let us come
to You.

Amen.

In the Arms of the Savior

And newly born
the lamb struggles
to stand
to lift itself
into God's sweet air.
But the lamb
keeps focus,
staring at the Shepherd,
rises
and trembling, begins
to walk.
The Shepherd smiles,
and before long,
in loving tenderness,
having been raised and
strengthened
by being with the other
sheep, guided by
our Shepherd
begins to run,
jump,
soar
with all Grace
having been raised
in the Savior's Arms.

Help Others

When you see someone
in need
forget your fears
and help them
and the Presence of
God will overwhelm you.

God's Eyes

Suddenly
the Light of Christ
will fill your life
you and your family will
be filled with love,
respect,
joy,
and peace.
God seeks you,
invites you
to accept His Love
so that when you are called
you will go to Him,
tears flowing,
and confessing your sins.
Accepting Christ into your heart
you will be saved,
and prayerfully
your family too
will be called.
What joy,
what happiness,
what love
can fill us
when courage lifts us
into God's eyes.

Your Gift

God's
many gifts
overwhelm.

Gather yourself
in His Word
and move
forward
using His gifts,

your gift,

to win souls
for Christ.

We the Church

Elsewhere they are working,
working
on the problems of mankind.

But we the church lead,
we pray,
today, this day,
gathered round with extended hands
praying for victory
in Jesus Christ.
May we be showered
with the blood of the Lamb.

Amen!

Humble Worship

Pray each day, each hour,
for miracles are needed
and worship is
of a humble, loving
Spirit.

Our Lord and Savior

In the garden
   was Christ—
tormented in prayer,
desperately
            seeking His Father—
and He asked
         "Watch and pray,"
Yet the men
             closest to Him
             who loved Him
fell asleep.
Jesus found them.
 "Wake… Watch… You must pray."
Yet again, as He sought His Father,
     those who loved Him so
            fell asleep.

We are weak— the flesh is
                  weak.
But when Jesus found them
     in kindness, He said
"Sleep… sleep…
               take your rest."
This is our Lord Christ:
His loving-kindness,
His forgiveness—
That makes us whole.

Destroy Satan

Christ defeated Satan on the cross.

Let us not be
confused in these days. Lord.
Destroy all evil.
Push Satan away.
Push him out of the world, Jesus.

Heal all of us,
come into our hearts.

Destroy Satan.

Amen!

God Breathed

God laid His hand
on earth
and then breathed
His Spirit
into the form
to create us.
We are filled
with God's Spirit
within us,
through us,
and when we
love one another
and worship Him,
we are in His image.
Christ confirmed
this when He said,
"Love one another
as I have loved you."[3]

3. John 13:34 NKJV.

Revival

Against the forces of destiny
lift our hearts
with purpose
allow revolution
from God's revival
to reach
the heights of the Universe.

Lost

What joy is there
in standing in line
in colors as all others
as mere men try to drown
individuality
try to drown our
uniqueness the beauty of a soul
in a mold of
be this for us
be lost for us
follow rules wc give you
forget freedom,
comply with our ways
forget God.

Darkness into Light

Falling to our knees
    tears streaming down
as we bow our heads
   and pray for God
to give Light
    to the darkness of
            our day.

Amen.

Essence

Into the soft realm
we exist
where there is choice
where we love freedom
as all love
having been made
by God's Breath
breathed into each of us
formed of flesh and spirit

and in the battle of our essence
we choose
Light or darkness

Jesus is the Light of the world
and we have
been created
to choose in complete freedom
Light
or sadly, Darkness

I choose Light
I choose Jesus
I choose love, peace
transformation
from a being of this world
to a being of God's Presence

to move into the Light
leaving darkness behind

and in that Presence
the Holy Spirit guides me
in pure love and joy

yes, in Your name, Jesus
You are the Light of the world.

Amen.

Lift Them Upward

Reach for the emptiness
  in your heart,
lift it up in prayers
              for others.
Reach often
      without pause,
reach
  as your prayers
     transform
in a pattern,
  in richness,
    in humbleness,
that gathers round
those you are praying for
and hold them gently in your arms.

  Lift them upward
where they can be filled,
where they can become truth,
where God transforms.

Grace

Lost in darkness
pray
seek the Light
seek Jesus
and your life
will be awakened
transformed
uplifted
saved
rejoice
Praise God
that the darkness is gone
and
Eternal Grace
is yours.

The Hurt Heart

Who can hurt
a small child?
No one unless
they possess
a hurt and hardened heart.
Pray for the child,
pray for the one who
hurts the child.
Pray for all hurt people
that they might realize God's Love
and, in doing so,
transform into a
child of God.

Victory

Fall on your knees
and flood the coals of hell
with the victory of the Holy Spirit!

Forever Found

lifting up
hearts
flying high
further
further
into the skies
upward
upward
stars breaking
into our eyes
as earth's sweet horizon
blue seas
drift from God's eyes
into our eyes

Praise Him
Praise Him
salvation is ours
given freely
on this soft blue
planet
lost in God's
magnificent universe
where we who are saved
are forever found.

Jesus

If you are walking
'round
and not being with God
read, pray, attend
until you find the blessed hum of
Jesus, Jesus, Jesus

in your mind...

in your essence...

in your soul.

God's Heart

Pray into the softness
    of all eternity
Pray to touch our Lord
Pray to remain close to His Heart
that we may do His will
    to love and touch others
        to lift them up in prayer
Pray into the softness
    of all presence, His Presence
Pray for all
    that they will be saved
Pray, pray for revival
    for the salvation of all
Pray into the softness
        of all eternity
Pray into God's Heart
            Pray.

Witness

If there is life,
If there is breath
In the other
They can be saved.

Waiting for you
Waiting for the Good News!

God Loves Each of Us

it is
in each
of us
God's Love

keep this in your heart
that God
loves
each of us
fully
completely
each of us
in His heart
sweet love
through grace given
through grace received.

Gather

Saved, we should
all gather
upon our knees
and thank Jesus
for all we have—

eternal joy—

being blessed by His Grace,
forever His.

Lifted Heart

Give your heart to Jesus,
lift it into the clouds,
feel the sin falling away.

It is
and will ever be
a new day
where grace is always
with you
and your praises
will ever lift you.

Angels are present,
encouraging you
to save others through Jesus,
to stop their human fall.

The judgment now
that might have befallen you
in Heaven
will be recalled.
Praise Jesus!
Worship Him
as your heart is lifted high
into Heaven.
Far above,
far above
earth's sky.

Thank You Lord Jesus

Lord Jesus
thank you for all
Your blessings
especially
suffering for us on the cross
for rising on the third day
for loving us
thank You Jesus
for eternal life.

Amen.

The Holy Bible

The Grace of God is flowing
in the name of our Savior
Jesus Christ...

Fall on your knees and pray
that all be saved
that all around you
in communion fall together
in a prayer of unity...

following the written Word of God
the Holy Bible.

God's Love

There is no other
love than God's love
so if you seek love
if you seek kindness
if you seek forgiveness
Seek Christ
for all love
all love
comes from the light
of the Savior
Jesus
Jesus Christ!

Amen!

Blessings Flow

Blessings flow
dreamers dream
speakers speak
prayers pray
but without Jesus' sacrifice
all is lost
without asking Jesus into your heart
nothing is nothing

so if you believe with all your heart
Jesus is the only Son of the living God
ask Him into your heart
confess your sins
Then,

blessings will flow
dreamers will dream
speakers will speak
prayers will pray

and in His name, Jesus,
God hears, God Blesses.

God's Sweet Presence

The angry web
of angry people
who blame God
often, in their hardness
stubbornness
can trap
children in the hate
flowing from confusion
if you suffer
if you feel anger at God
somehow blame Him for
your situation
your life
find help
seek God in prayer
seek God in counseling
seek God
until you feel His
warm, sweet love
holding you, caring for you
and you know the
difficulties of your life
were whispers of evil
now, in faith, you can lead
lead your family
and your children
to God
to His sweet Presence.

Faith, Hope, and Love

Pray in thankfulness
    for all the blessings
Christ gives us:
Faith, Hope, and Love
    every morning,
        each day,
        in the coming darkness.
Be thankful for
    all who love us
    and all we love,
but most of all
    for the presence of God
    that is with us always
through all
    even the night.

Invite Him In

Open
Open your heart
Jesus loves you
loves you
you
forget all the
despair
the emptiness
in your life
feel the fullness
of His Love
He loves you
fully
completely
He chose the cross
for He loved you
sacrificed His blood for you
Invite Him into your life
be saved
accept His Love
His Grace
His Forgiveness.

Run to Jesus

Run to Jesus!
        Run with all your might.
And rejoice,
                rejoice,
                        rejoice!
For the Lord is your Savior.

In the Drift of His Love

When sadness strikes,
touches deeply in your soul,
reach for your Bible
and open anywhere.
Read God's anointed words
then fall and pray
for God's blessings
to calm your world
and in your heart
ask Him to shoulder your pain.

Lift your heart

in faith

as the world relaxes

and your heart steadies,

calm in the drift of His Love

God's Love.

Prayer of Salvation

In this moment
of harmony
in the name of Jesus Christ
through His Grace
let us pray
and claim
that all who seek Him will come
and in His name confess their sins
and profess that Jesus Christ
is the one and only begotten Son of God

then turn away from Satan and evil
and rejoice in the name of the Lord

Amen!
Praise God!

About the Author

Anton Knox Elder graduated from the University of West Georgia with a B.A. in psychology and a minor in philosophy, later acquiring a M.A. in psychology. Soon after graduating he worked as a psychologist at Gracewood State School and Hospital in Augusta, GA and later transferred to Ogeechee M.R. Services in Waynesboro, GA. In 1993 Knox was in a severe car accident, which resulted in short term memory loss and chronic pain. Knox and his family were devastated.

Knox had written poetry since the age of twelve and had a unique ability to deeply touch the heart of his readers. He was fascinated by the universe and everything in it, which came out in his writing. However, for almost twenty years after the car accident Knox was unable to write and could only read for brief periods. While struggling with the loss of a dynamic career and a complete change of life style, Knox developed a personal relationship with Christ and began to receive healing. Suddenly poetry began to flow again out of his close relationship with the Lord. A few years later his wife, Susan, went through the many notebooks of poems and put them together to form this book, naming it after Knox's favorite poem, "Against Starlight." He gives credit to Susan for the creation of this book and praises God for the gift of writing.

Knox can be contacted at: againststarlight@gmail.com.

More Titles by 5 Fold Media

Journey of Faith
by Karen Hinman and Lori Lucarelli
$34.95
ISBN: 978-1-936578-38-2

Journey of Faith by Karen Hinman and Lori Lucarelli combines poetry and photography in a unique literary adventure. In the summer of 2009, Karen Hinman was inspired to embark on a year-long disciplined journey to write a series of poems addressing sensitive issues that challenged her faith and spawned spiritual growth in her life.

For Lori Lucarelli, God has always used photography as a type of therapy: uplifting, encouraging, and a reminder of how much He is involved in everyday life. As Karen and Lori began to collaborate on this project, it proved to be a divinely orchestrated partnership, as each poem and corresponding picture was matched up by God's hand.

The Psalms, Poetry on Fire
The Passion Translation
by Dr. Brian Simmons
$19.00
ISBN: 978-1-936578-28-3

The Psalms, Poetry on Fire find the words that express our deepest and strongest emotions. The Psalms will turn your sighing into singing and your trouble into triumph. No matter what you may be going through in your life, the Psalms have a message for you! As you read these 150 poetic masterpieces, your heart will be stirred to worship God in greater ways.

Author Brian Simmons shares, "The Psalms are meant to do to you what they did to David; they will bring you from your cave of despair into the glad presence of the King who likes you just the way you are." It truly is Poetry on Fire!

Like 5 Fold Media on Facebook, follow us on Twitter!

CPSIA information can be obtained at www.ICGtesting.com
Printed in the USA
LVOW02s0119161113

361554LV00009B/892/P